A Little Thyme
& A PINCH OF RHYME

A Little Thyme
& A PINCH OF RHYME

A COOKBOOK IN HAIKU & SONNETS

Stephen Cramer

WIND RIDGE BOOKS

Shelburne, Vermont USA 05482

Also by Stephen Cramer:

Shiva's Drum

Tongue & Groove

From the Hip (A Concise History of Hip Hop in Sonnets)

Bone Music

For Joanna, who has taught me so much, not just about sustenance but also how to sustain. She also makes a pretty mean kimchi.

Published by Wind Ridge Books of Vermont,
an imprint of the Voices of Vermonters Publishing Group, Inc.
PO Box 595
Shelburne, Vermont 05482
www.windridgebooksofvt.com

Printed in the United States of America

The Menu

Introduction

I learned a lot while writing this book. First & foremost I learned that you have to press the *Option* & the *Shift* keys at the same time, & then hold down the 8, and that gives you the "degrees" sign. It seems like an intense process for something that comes out like this: °. But still, it feels somehow miraculous when it happens. Second, I learned that my computer doesn't know how to spell *arugula*. Shocking. No, computer, I am not trying to spell "argyle" or "arguable." Some other ingredients that the computer doesn't recognize: *chipotle, samosa, Kalamata, tabouli,* & *tahini*. Some of its suggestions for these words include: *chapter, Samoa, calamity, tubful,* & *taming*, none of which sound particularly appetizing to me. It's almost as if the computer doesn't eat at all.

I know you want to get cooking, but I have a few quick notes about the form of this book. At first I wanted the manuscript to be made up completely of sonnets. But then I found that I had to make the ingredient lists into haiku, mostly because very few words rhyme with "tablespoon" or "teaspoon" (let's face it: very few ingredients are maroon, & you can only mention baboons so many times in a single manuscript). Also, in the interest of syllable count, the occasional ingredient list is slightly out of order. And lastly, sometimes in this book you'll find that the word "oil" is one syllable, and sometimes you'll find it's two, according to the recipe's needs. It's all about the recipe.

—S.C.

A Little Thyme & a Pinch of Rhyme

Breakfast

Eggs Italiano with Zucchini & Tomato

Ingredients: 1
tablespoon of olive oil,
1/4 cup of

minced onion, 1 clove
garlic, 1 diced zucchini,
2 diced tomatoes,

1/4 cup of
chopped basil, 1 tablespoon
of vinegar (best

to use balsamic),
1/2 teaspoon of salt &
1/8 teaspoon of

black pepper, 4 eggs,
1/4 cup of freshly
grated Parmesan

Directions: Boil two inches of water

in a large pan. (Inches is a basic

measurement for liquids, right?) Meanwhile, heat your

oil in a skillet. Add the onion & garlic,

& sauté for 4 minutes. Next, stir

in the zucchini & tomatoes, & keep stirring

to combine. Cook for 8 minutes. Add the vinegar,

basil, salt, & pepper. Bring the boiling

water (if it's not boiling yet, you

either A) need to buy a new stove or

B) forgot to turn on the burner) down to

a simmer. Slip each cracked egg into the water,

& cook for 4 minutes. Transfer the zucchini

mixture to plates with the eggs, & top with cheese.

Skillet Home Fries with Hot Sauce

Ingredients: 2
pounds of potatoes (Yukon
Gold work best in this

one) halved lengthwise then
sliced a half an inch thick, 2
tablespoons of oil,

1 green pepper cut
into thin, inch-long pieces,
1 onion coarsely

chopped, 1 teaspoon of
salt, a few twists of freshly
ground black peppercorns

**Ingredients for
hot sauce:** 1 cup vinegar,
20 hot peppers,

2 cloves of garlic,
1 teaspoon of salt & 1
teaspoon of sugar

(The hot sauce part is
optional, but only if
you hate your taste buds)

Directions: Place the potatoes in

a pot & cover them with cold

water. Bring the water to a boil. (I've often

followed recipes that have told

me to bring the *pot* to a boil. *That's crazy,*

I always think: *a boiling pot.* So um...

let's just boil the water this time.) Anyway,

once boiling, turn the heat to medium,

& cook the potatoes for 15 more

minutes until they're heated through but still

firm. Drain. Preheat a large skillet over

medium heat, then add 1 tablespoon of oil.

Stir the oil to coat the skillet. When it's hot,

add the potatoes & stir to coat. Let

them cook for 5 minutes, or until

lightly browned. Toss & let them cook for

another 10 minutes. Add the onion, green pepper,

salt, pepper, & the other tablespoon of oil.

Cook for 7 more minutes, stirring

often, until the peppers & onions

are soft.

The potatoes are best when doused in

the following **hot sauce recipe:** bring

the vinegar to a boil in a small

sauce pan. Drop in the garlic & peppers,

& boil until the vegetables are tender.

Transfer to a blender & wait until

cool. Blend with the salt & sugar. I like to

multiply this recipe by ten. So will you.

Vegan Broccoli Quiche Unleashed

Ingredients: 2 tablespoons of olive oil, 1 yellow onion

finely chopped, 2 minced garlic cloves, 3 cups finely chopped broccoli, 1

teaspoon of dried thyme, 1 teaspoon of turmeric, 1 teaspoon of salt,

1/4 teaspoon pepper, 1/2 cup cashews, 1 teaspoon mustard,

1 pound of tofu, 1 pie crust (bought from the store or homemade. For the

latter, please refer to the cherry pie recipe on page 82).

Directions: Preheat the oven

to 350°. Heat a skillet over

medium heat, & sauté the onion

& garlic in the olive oil for

3 minutes. Add the broccoli, salt,

thyme, turmeric, & pepper. While this cooks (for

10 minutes) walk to your stereo & put

on a few choice cuts of Art Pepper.

(Nothing says sizzling onions & thyme quite

like *Las Cuevas de Mario* or

Smack Up. Let the music start your day off *right*.)

Now, put the cashews into a food processor.

Then, if you can bear to interrupt Art Pepper,

pulse them into fine crumbs. If not, either

crank up your stereo to

11, or B) wait till the song's over. (Choose A.)

Add the mustard & crumble in the tofu.

Process until smooth. When the broccoli

mixture is done, add a cup of it to

the processor & pulse until just

combined. (Don't over-mix.) Transfer the tofu

mixture to a bowl & add the rest

of the broccoli. Stir to combine.

With a spatula, scrape this mixture

into a pie crust. (You went out & bought one,

didn't you?) Bake for 40 minutes. Let cool for

20 minutes, or as long as you can

stand it, before you start digging in.

Practically Perfect Potato Pancakes

Ingredients: 4
pounds of potatoes (Yukon
Gold will do the trick),

1/3 cup of
canola oil, 1/4
teaspoon turmeric,

1 teaspoon of salt,
1 tablespoon of mustard
seeds, 1 chopped onion,

1 cup diced carrot,
3 minced cloves of garlic, 1
tablespoon finely

chopped fresh ginger, 2
teaspoons of ground cumin, 2
teaspoons red pepper

flakes, 3/4 cup
of peas, 1/4 cup of
flour, oil for cooking

Directions: Place the potatoes in

a pot & cover with cold water.

Bring to a boil, then lower the heat & simmer

for 20 minutes, until you've been

mesmerized by the potatoes (or until they're

tender.) Meanwhile, heat the oil in a skillet,

then add the mustard seeds & let

them pop. (Unless you're wearing goggles, cover

the pot during this part. Trust me.) Then

add the onion & carrot, & sauté

for about 10 more minutes. When they

are soft, add the garlic, ginger, cumin,

& red pepper flakes. Gently cook for another

5 minutes. Once the potatoes are

done, drain them & return them to

the pot. Add the oil, turmeric,

& salt, & mash the mixture with a fork

until it's relatively smooth.

Stir in the onions & carrots, the peas,

& the flour. Mix well, then let it sit for

10 minutes. Once cooled, roll the mixture

into Ping-Pong sized balls. Then flatten these

out to form cakes. Preheat a large skillet

over medium heat & add a thin layer

of oil. Cook each cake for 3 or

4 minutes on each side, or until it

is light brown. Arrange them on a plate.

Remove goggles, & *bon appétit*!

Haiku to Dancing Mustard Seeds

Some compare you to
the kingdom of heaven &
speak of birds lodging

in the branches of
the tree you could become. But
I believe you're just

as happy here in
my old, flame-stained pot, jumping
& dancing about

in the vegetable
kingdom's inexplicable
version of rapture.

The Only Tofu Scram Recipe You'll Ever Need

Ingredients: 1
tablespoon of olive oil,
1 chopped onion, 3

cloves of minced garlic,
a pound of drained firm tofu,
1/4 cup of

nutritional yeast,
2 tablespoons of freshly
squeezed lemon juice, 2

teaspoons ground cumin,
2 teaspoon of dried thyme, 1
teaspoon paprika,

1 teaspoon of
turmeric, 1 teaspoon of
salt (or to your taste)

Directions: Heat the oil in a skillet over

medium heat & sauté the onions

for 3 minutes. Add the garlic & sauté for

2 minutes more. Now add the cumin,

the thyme, the paprika, the turmeric,

& the salt. Crumble in the tofu

& stir. Cook for 15 minutes; mix

occasionally. Add the lemon juice

& the nutritional yeast, & stir it

all up. Transfer to a plate, & chow down. NOTE:

This just might be my favorite

breakfast dish of all time, but please oh please don't

attempt to substitute eggs for the tofu.

Ask Bob. He's tried it. So you don't have to.

Blissful* Banana & Berry Smoothie

Ingredients: 1
frozen banana, 1 cup
berries (try a mix

of some blueberries,
strawberries & raspberries,
though skip the last if

you don't like the seeds'
crunch), 1 tablespoon syrup
(apologies to

Tia Jemima,
but she just can't cut it here),
1/2 cup of milk

(cow's milk or, even
better, rice milk) 1/2 cup
of a rich yogurt

* **Note:** If you found no
bliss after eating this, you
must have made it wrong.

Directions: Peel & chop up the banana.

Drop it into a blender with your favorite

mix of fresh or frozen berries. Pour in the

milk. (Use rice milk if you want to make it

vegan, or use cow's milk to make it more

palatable if you happen to be

serving baby cows.) Add the yogurt. Blend for

30 seconds, & pour into 3

chilled glasses. If you're like me, you'll slurp

this up with a spoon. But if chunky

isn't your thing, simply add cold water

to your desired consistency

& use a curlicue straw for that extra flair,

& invite the neighborhood kids to share.

Lunch

Orzo Salad of Awesomeness

Ingredients: 1
& a 1/2 cups of orzo,
1/3 cup of chopped

sun-dried tomatoes
in oil, 4 tablespoons
of olive oil,

1/4 cup of
vinegar (I like to use
balsamic), 1/2

cup Kalamata
olives coarsely chopped, & 1
cup of finely chopped

lettuce, 1/2 cup
of pine nuts, 1/2 cup of
chopped basil, 1/2

cup of grated Parm,
3 minced garlic cloves, freshly
ground pepper, & salt

Directions: Bring a pot of water to

a boil & cook the orzo for 9 minutes.

Be sure not to overcook (unless you

only like pasta salad when it

has the consistency of overdone oatmeal).

Drain & pour into a large-ish bowl.

Add the sun-dried tomatoes, oil & vinegar while

the orzo is still hot. Cover the whole

dish, & let it sit until cooled. (Stir

intermittently.) Add all the other

ingredients to the orzo mixture,

& season with salt & pepper.

Note: This recipe also pairs well with a
splash more balsamic & a little feta.

Haiku to Orzo

Orzo (your name is
from the Italian word
for *barley*) you are

the smallest pasta
on my shelves (though on some you're
a close second to

pastina). I love
you in hot soups, & I love
you in cold salads,

but mostly I love
the way your name feels in my
mouth, & I could say

you all day long &
not need much else to happen:
orzo, orzo, orzo...

Truly Unruly* Tabouli

Ingredients: Some
use bulgur for this, but trust
me, try 1/2 cup

of uncooked quinoa
instead, 4 tablespoons of
olive oil, 2

diced tomatoes, 1
small diced onion, 3 garlic
cloves minced, 1 large bunch

of chopped parsley, 2
tablespoons lemon juice, salt
& pepper to taste

* Actually, it's
only unruly if you
chop the parsley too

coarsely. If you have
a dull knife, be sure to keep
a mirror handy

so that you can check
your teeth frequently for the
errant parsley speck.

Directions: First of all, yes, this can be

spelled as Tabouli, Tabbouleh, or Taboli.

Now that that's cleared up, bring a pot of water

to a boil. Lower the heat & pour

in the quinoa. Cook for 15 minutes

or until it's done. Place the quinoa in a

bowl & stir in the olive oil. In

another bowl, mix together the onion,

tomatoes, garlic, parsley, & lemon

juice. Pour this into the quinoa, &

stir to combine. Add salt & pepper. Either

serve in bowls or, if you're slightly more

daring, roll into lettuce leaves. Then you'll know:

there's nothing quite like a Lebanese burrito.

It's All Greek to Me* Salad

Ingredients: 1
small jar of artichoke hearts,
2 cucumbers halved

lengthwise & cut up
into half moons, 2 hefty
tomatoes cut in

a large dice, 1 diced
red pepper, 1 diced yellow
onion, 21

pitted olives (I
think Kalamata work the
best), 8 tablespoons

of olive oil, 5
tablespoons of vinegar,
1 tablespoon dried

oregano, 1
tablespoon of lemon juice,
1 cup feta cheese

*Actually, Salad,
I fully "get" you. You're like
my tongue's first language.

Directions: In a large bowl, simply

    arrange the artichokes, tomatoes,

& cucumbers (I know, dear history

    buffs: the tomato didn't make it to

Greece until the 1800s, but work with me

    here), the pepper, the olives, & onion.

(Okay, while we're being honest, we

    should say that the Greeks probably didn't even

chop up their veggies much at all until

    the early 20th century, but trust

    me... that revolution was for the best.)

Then, in a bowl, whisk together the oil,

vinegar, oregano, & lemon juice. Pour the

dressing on the salad. On top, crumble the feta.

Haiku to Kalamata Olives

Oh, most perfect of
cooking olives, you are named
after a city

in Peloponnesia.
But to me you conjure not
some ancient Greek war

just purple's deepest
& most perfect shade cut with
a briny grey. Each

"a" in your name is
an olive of its own, stemmed
& with a pit of

white space, a pit that
I would keep swallowing whole
again & again.

Mushroom, Tomato, & Quinoa Stuffed Peppers

Ingredients: 1 tablespoon of olive oil, 1 cup of finely

chopped onion, 2 minced cloves of garlic, 4 cups of finely chopped mushrooms,

2-3 teaspoons chili powder, 1 teaspoon salt, 15 ounces

of crushed tomatoes (canned is fine here), 1/2 cup of quinoa, 4 large

red bell peppers, 1 15-ounce can of black beans, 1 teaspoon syrup

Directions: In a medium saucepan,

cook the onion in the oil over medium

heat for 5 minutes, until it becomes,

as some recipes say, "clear." (Do onions

ever *really* get clear? Hmm.) Throw the

garlic & mushrooms in. Sauté for another

5 minutes. Stir in the chili powder

& the salt. Add the half a cup of quinoa

& 1 cup of crushed tomatoes. (Did you hear me?

Just 1 of the cups!) Add a quarter

cup of water. Lower the heat, cover,

& simmer until the quinoa's done (20

minutes or so.) Meanwhile, boil some water

in a large pot. Cut the tops off the peppers

& remove the seeds. Boil the peppers

      for 5 minutes, then drain. Mix the beans &

maple syrup into the quinoa mixture,

      then stuff the peppers with the filling & stand

them up in a baking dish. If they refuse

      to stand up, flatten the bottoms with your

knife (& next time make sure to choose

      flat-bottomed peppers). Lastly, pour

the remaining crushed tomatoes over

      the peppers & bake at 375°

for 20 minutes. Plate the peppers,

      topping with a sprinkle of Parmesan cheese

if you like. (For a tasty, dairy-free option,

try a mixture of salt & ground almonds.)

Wheat Berry & Black Bean Chili

Ingredients: 2
tablespoons of olive oil,
1 chopped onion, 1

chopped yellow pepper,
4 minced cloves of garlic, 2
teaspoons of chili

powder, 2 teaspoons
of cumin, 1 teaspoon of
dried oregano,

1/2 teaspoon salt,
1/2 teaspoon of freshly
ground pepper, 2 drained

15-ounce cans of
black beans, one 28-ounce
can of tomatoes

(crushed), 3 chipotle
peppers in adobo sauce
(finely chopped), 2 cups

of vegetable broth,
2 teaspoons syrup, 2
cups wheat berries (cooked),

2 tablespoons lime
juice, 1 cup cilantro, 1
diced avocado

Directions: Heat the olive oil in

a large pot. Add the onion, pepper,

garlic, chili powder, oregano, cumin,

salt, & pepper. Cook the veggies until tender,

about 5 minutes. Now add the zing:

chipotle, tomatoes, broth & syrup. Turn

the heat to high & bring

the mixture to a boil. Then turn it back down

& simmer for 25 minutes.

Stir in the wheat berries (Mmm, I love

me some berries. Oh, wait...) & cook it

down for another 5 minutes. Remove

from the heat & stir in the lime juice. Cilantro

makes a nice garnish. So does avocado.

Garlicky Broccoli with Tofu(ie?)

Ingredients: 2
cups of vegetable stock, 3
heads of broccoli

chopped into bite-sized
pieces, 5 minced cloves garlic,
1/4 cup of

soy sauce (or better
yet, tamari), 1 teaspoon
of powdered ginger,

1 teaspoon of red
pepper flakes, 2 tablespoons
of brown sugar, 2

tablespoons of corn-
starch, 1 block of firm tofu
chopped into bite-sized

pieces, 1 or 2
tablespoons of olive or
vegetable oil

Directions: In a pan, bring the veggie

stock to a boil. Add the garlic, ginger,

tamari, red pepper flakes, & sugar.

Meanwhile, dissolve the corn starch in 3

tablespoons of cold water. In a skillet,

cook the broccoli in the oil for

5 minutes. Add the garlic mixture

to the broccoli, & simmer it

over medium heat for 8 minutes.

Add the corn starch mixture & the tofu,

& stir to combine. Cook for 2

more minutes, until the sauce thickens.

Serve over brown rice. Without a doubt,

this'll be your new definition of "take out."

Grilled Pizza with Roasted Red Peppers, Olives & Arugula

Ingredients: 1
recipe of (or pre-bought)
dough, enough cornmeal

for sprinkling, olive
oil, a cup of tomato
sauce, a cup of jarred

red roasted peppers,
drained & cut into 1/2 inch
bites, 1/3 cup of

pitted & coarsely
chopped Kalamata olives,
1 cup of shredded

Parmesan cheese, 2
teaspoons of chopped rosemary,
1 chopped medium

red onion, 2 cups
of arugula, & salt
& pepper to taste

Directions: Preheat the oven to

500°. Sprinkle the counter

with cornmeal. Then, with a rolling pin, start to roll out your

dough. Brush the top with oil, & bake for a few

minutes until the underside is browned.

Remove the dough from the oven & flip

so that the brown side is facing up.

Spoon on the sauce & scatter peppers & olives around

the top. Sprinkle with rosemary, arugula,

& onion rings. Then spread the Parmesan

cheese over those. Bake for 7

minutes. Add salt & pepper to taste, & slice the

pie into 2-inch wide strips. (Believe me, these

will taste better than the standard isosceles.)

Snacks

Tomato & Black Bean Salsa

Ingredients: 4 cups of chopped tomatoes, 2 drained cans of black beans,

1 diced medium onion, 1 jalapeño (finely chopped), 1/2

cup of cilantro (chopped), 2 finely diced cloves of garlic, salt to taste,

black pepper to taste, 6 tablespoons lime juice, 1 tablespoon olive oil

Directions: In a bowl, mix together

the tomatoes, onions, garlic, black beans,

jalapeño, cilantro, pepper,

& salt. (Don'tcha just love recipes

where the only tools you really need

are a bowl & a spoon? This quality

makes this salsa a perfect recipe

for a last minute get together. Simply

add beer, chips, music, & *boom*: you've got yourself a

party.) Oh, & add the lime juice

& olive oil. Mix well. Serve with tortilla

chips & a side of guacamole. Best if used

with recommended music: an upbeat

Stan Getz circa 1963.

Pico de Gallo Salsa & Tortilla Chips

Ingredients: 4
large tomatoes, 4 chopped green
onions, 3 finely

chopped jalapeño
peppers, 2 tablespoons of
vegetable oil,

1/2 cup of chopped
cilantro, 2 tablespoons
lime juice, salt to taste

Directions: Blend all the ingredients

in a food processor until coarsely chopped,

& there: you have your salsa. Now, since we've got

some time left in this week's show, let's

talk about the name of this recipe.

Pico de Gallo literally means... (pause

for translation...) "rooster's beak," so named because

when you eat it, it's so spicy

that it feels like the salsa is pecking your

tongue. Now, that may not sound super

appetizing to some folks. But I assure

you, these are highly trained roosters.

So dip a chip into this perfect snack,

& do you best to bite the rooster back.

Haiku to the Jalapeño

Oh, most wonderful
of peppers, you who are named
after Xalapa,

Veracruz (the first
city in which your kind was
cultivated), you

& the cayenne are
tied for first in my tongue's long
list of favorite

peppers. Your heat is
inviting, perhaps because
so few of us let

you ripen past the
color of *go*, & into
that of the stop sign.

Tomato-Basil Bruschetta

Ingredients: 1
loaf of sliced French bread (if it's
a day old, then all

the better), 2 cups
of chopped tomatoes, 1/2
cup of basil (minced),

1 tablespoon of
olive oil, 3 finely diced
cloves of garlic, salt

& pepper to taste,
4 tablespoons of freshly
grated Parmesan

Directions: Preheat the oven to 400°.

Arrange the slices of French bread

      (which is the best thing since itself, or so

      they say) on an oven sheet & grill on both

sides until light brown & crispy.

      Then make the topping: combine your

tomatoes, the basil, the sea

      salt, the olive oil, garlic, & the pepper.

Top the grilled bread with the tomato mixture,

      & sprinkle on the Parmesan

cheese. Place on a baking sheet & return

      to the oven for 4 minutes, or until the cheese on

top melts. & there's your antipasti (Italian

for, "instead of the meal" * with a glass of wine).

* **Note:** Actually,
more than 1 or 2 people
have told me that it

means "before the meal,"
but who can really trust a
hungry Italian?

Bob's Black Bean Hummus with Pita Triangles

Ingredients: 1
15 ounce can of black beans,
1 15 ounce can

of chickpeas, 7
teaspoons hot sesame oil,
2 minced garlic cloves,

4 teaspoons cumin,
1 bunch fresh cilantro (chopped),
3 tablespoons of

lemon juice, 6 to
7 teaspoons tamari,
1/2 teaspoon salt,

1/2 teaspoon of
black pepper, 1/2 a cup
tahini, either

homemade or store bought
pita bread sliced into 6
to 8 triangles.

Directions: Place all but the sesame

oil & cilantro in a blender

& pulse, adding a bit of water

until you've got the right consistency

(you want it fairly smooth with a few solid

pieces). Now transfer the mixture to a bowl

& add the oil & cilantro.

Mix, then taste to see that it's properly salted

& peppered. This recipe pairs perfectly

with the poetry of Philip Levine.

(Try *What Work Is*: the title poem, or "Gin.")

Pablo Neruda, though he may also be

excellent, can be too floral for this recipe. But

as always, serve according to your palate.

Hippie Popcorn

Ingredients: 1 tablespoon of vegetable oil, a cup of

popcorn kernels, a few splashes of soy sauce, & nutritional yeast

Directions: pour the oil into a small

pot over medium heat. When the oil's hot

enough to sizzle, pour in the kernels

& swirl to coat the bottom of the pot

with oil, then cover it tightly.

When the popping subsides, remove from the heat

& pour into a bowl. Pour the soy

sauce over the top, then sprinkle (be

generous) with nutritional yeast. Ideally

the "nooch" sticks to the soy sauce & doesn't filter

down to the bottom of the bowl. This recipe

goes well with both *The Prisoner*

of Azkaban (if you're hanging out

with a young crowd) or *Citizen Kane* (if you're not).

Warning: have extra
ingredients on hand, 'cause
you *will* want to make

more. Especially
if the movie is long (or
if your partner hogs).

Haiku to Nutritional Yeast

Nutritional yeast,
you are oh so much better
than you sound (though your

name is perhaps a
touch more appetizing than
sacchoromyces

cerevisiae,
the organism of but
a single cell that

you're made from). Some would
say you're nutty, some cheesy,
but few can argue

that you deliver
that unique *umami* taste
to the foods you grace.

Bonus Haiku to Umami

Umami, you are
the fifth basic taste (along
with sweet, sour, bitter,

& salty). Way back
when, in 1908, you
were "discovered" by

a Japanese chef
named Kikunae Ikeda:
glutamic acid,

he found, gave some foods
a certain special something,
but to the untrained

ear, *glutamic* &
acid tend to sound fairly
unappetizing

(for more on the
fine art of renaming food,
please see previous

haiku), so he dubbed
it *Umami* (the Japanese
word for *delicious*).

Joey's Seed Crackers

Ingredients: 1 cup of flax seeds, 1/2 cup chia seeds, 1/2

cup sesame seeds, 1/2 cup sunflower seeds, 1/2 cup of hemp

hearts, (feel free to sub any seeds here) a handful of crumbled nori

Directions: pour the chia & flax

seeds into a bowl & cover with water. Relax

for 10 minutes, until the chia

has the consistency of egg whites (I hear ya,

it seems impossible, but you have to trust

me here). Mix in the rest of the seeds, then just

add the crumbled nori. Pour the seed

mixture onto a parchment paper-lined cookie

sheet & spread until it's cracker-thin.

Bake at 350° for 15-

20 minutes until the giant cracker

is dry. Flip & bake for another

10 minutes. Remove from oven & break

into rustic, non-geometrical shapes.

Dinner

Quick! Let's Whip Up Some of That Pasta with Radicchio & Cream!

Ingredients: 2-
3 tablespoons of butter,
2 large-ish heads of

radicchio, 1
15 ounce can of kidney
beans, 3/4 cup

heavy cream, 1/2
cup of grated Parmesan
cheese, 1 pound pasta

(I like the way that
this sauce goes with rotini),
salt, grated pepper

Directions: Melt the butter in

       a large pot. Add the radicchio, & heat

gently until somewhat softened (about 7

       minutes). Season to taste with salt

& pepper. Stir in the heavy cream, the beans,

       & the Parmesan cheese. (Feel free

to add a bit more cheese or a splash more cream

       if your guests are particularly

charming.) Simmer until the sauce has thickened

       a bit. Meanwhile, cook the pasta *al*

dente (not *al Dante*, which I assume would

       mean, "scorched to hell"). Drain the pasta well

& add to the sauce, stirring to incorporate,

& serve with crusty bread on a heated plate.

Jesse's Sicilian Eggplant Parm

Ingredients: Have
enough olive oil for
frying, 2 small-to-

medium eggplants,
3-4 cups of finely
diced tomatoes (I

like to season those
with a few pinches of thyme
& some salt) 1/3

cup of freshly chopped
parsley, 1/2 cup breadcrumbs,
1/2 cup grated

Parmesan cheese, 5
cloves of garlic that you've chopped
into a fine dice

Directions: Slice the eggplants thin

    & fry in the oil. Then start to layer

    the dish in a non-metallic container

thus: first spread a layer of the eggplant on

the bottom. You'll want to overlap

    the slices of eggplant. (Contrary to belief,

"Parmigiana" doesn't refer to the type

    of cheese used in this recipe.

It really just means "in the style of Parma,"

    & some say it has more to do with layering than

the cheese used.) Cover the eggplant with the

    sauce. Shake on the breadcrumbs then the cheese. Then

sprinkle on parsley & garlic. Layer till you're

out of eggplant. Serve at room temperature.

Buen Provecho Zucchini Burritos

Ingredients: 2
tablespoons of olive oil,
1 cup of finely

chopped onion, 2 minced
cloves garlic, 3 medium
zucchini (shredded),

1 chopped bell pepper,
1 15 ounce can of black
beans, 1 cup salsa,

1/2 teaspoon of
ground cumin, 1/2 teaspoon
of cayenne pepper,

tortillas (a large,
warmed stack) & a cup or so of
shredded cheddar cheese

Directions: Heat the oil in a skillet,

then saute the garlic & onion

over medium heat for 5 minutes.

Stir in the shredded zucchini &

the red bell pepper, & cook for

10 minutes more. Stir in the beans, cumin,

salsa, & cayenne pepper. If you're

into bathing in zucchini juice, then

go ahead & roll a good cup of

the filling into the heated

tortillas now. If not, let it cook for 5

more minutes. (The latter is recommended.)

Sprinkle with cheese & roll up the burrito

as tight as you can. *¡Buen provecho!*

Magic Dhal

Ingredients: 1
cup of orange lentils, 1
coarsely chopped onion,

2 tablespoons of
margarine, 2 chopped garlic
cloves, 1 tablespoon

mustard seeds, 1 teaspoon
each of cumin, turmeric
& coriander,

1 teaspoon of salt,
1 cup canned diced tomatoes,
1/4 teaspoon

of ground black pepper,
1/4 teaspoon of red
hot pepper flakes, 2

yellow potatoes
cut up into small dice, 2
tablespoons lime juice

Directions: Melt the margarine

in a large pot or wok over

low heat. Add the garlic, mustard seeds, & onion,

& sauté for 3 minutes. Add the other

seasonings & sauté for 3

or 4 more minutes. Then add your

tomatoes, potatoes, split peas,

& enough water to cover. Simmer

until the potatoes & lentils

are tender. Then stir in the lime juice. Note:

Some will spell this recipe: "dal."

(The word comes from the Sanskrit verb "to split.")

But I prefer "dhal." (The extra h is

for "How awesome can a recipe be?") Serve with rice.

The Lost Shepherd's Pie

Ingredients: 5
large russet potatoes, 2
tablespoons of sour

cream, 1 egg, 2 cups
veggie broth, 1 tablespoon
of butter, 1

tablespoon olive
oil, one diced large onion,
one diced large carrot,

2 cups of peas, 2
cups of veggie crumbles, 2
tablespoons soy sauce

(or tamari), 2
teaspoons each of paprika
& dried parsley

Directions: In a large pot, boil

the potatoes. When tender (not you, dear

reader, the potatoes) drain & mash them all

up. Add 1 cup of veggie broth, the sour

cream, the egg, & the butter. Mix it

all until smooth. In a large pan,

heat the oil, then sauté the carrot

& onion until they're soft (7

or 8 minutes). Then add the peas, your

second cup of broth, & the veggie crumble. Stir

in the soy sauce. Transfer the mixture

to a casserole dish. Top with a layer

of potatoes. Top with paprika & parsley,

& bake for 20 minutes at 400°.

Cauliflower Bowl with Dragon Sauce

Ingredients: 3
tablespoons of olive oil,
1/2 cup (or

maybe two shakes more)
of nutritional yeast, (*nooch*
to all you hipsters

out there) 1/4
cup of peanut butter, 3
tablespoons syrup,

2 tablespoons of
tamari, 5 tablespoons
of water, 2 chopped

cloves of garlic, 1
block of firm tofu (14
oz) cut into cubes,

1 tablespoon of
vegetable oil, 1 large
head cauliflower

cut into bite-sized
pieces, 1 cup of uncooked
quinoa, water

Directions: For the dragon sauce (it's

not as dangerous as it sounds), mix

the nutritional yeast, peanut butter,

olive oil, maple syrup, water,

tamari, & garlic in a Ball jar, & shake

it up. Resist the urge to drink

this straight. (Or give in to the urge, as long as you

have enough ingredients to

make more). Heat the vegetable oil

in a skillet, & cook the tofu until

each side is lightly browned. On another

burner, bring a couple cups of water

to a boil & steam the cauliflower.

On your third & final burner

(you know you can never get that fourth one to
light) boil the quinoa in 2

cups of water until it's tender.
When the tofu, quinoa, & cauliflower

are done, find a nice blue bowl. (Trust me,
9 out of 10 food stylists agree

that blue best sets off this dish. Oh,
& those 9 have met in private quarters to

scoff at the 10th, whom they've decided has
always been a hack.) Now layer as

many tofu cubes as you like over your
quinoa, & pile on the cauliflower.

Drizzle with dragon sauce liberally,
& serve with chopsticks (or forks for the lazy).

Mushroom & Bok Choy Hotpot

Ingredients: 5
cups of vegetable broth, 2
tablespoons of fresh

chopped ginger, 2 minced
cloves of garlic, 2 teaspoons
of vegetable oil,

2 cups of trimmed &
coarsely chopped shiitake (or
heck, even button)

mushrooms, 1/4
teaspoon of red pepper flakes,
1 chopped bunch of bok

choy separated
into two piles: stems & greens,
4 ounces of rice

noodles, 1 package
of tofu cut into small
cubes, 5 teaspoons of

rice vinegar, 2
teaspoons tamari, & 1
of sesame oil

Directions: Combine the broth, ginger

& garlic in a large pot. Bring to a boil

then lower the heat & simmer

for 15 minutes. Meanwhile, heat the oil

in a skillet over medium

heat. Add the mushrooms & red pepper

flakes. Cook for 4 minutes. Add the stems

of the bok choy & cook for another 4

to 5 minutes. Add the mushroom mixture to

the broth. Then stir in the bok choy greens

& the tofu. Simmer until heated through.

Pour in the vinegar, tamari,

& sesame oil. Add the noodles & simmer the

dish for 2 minutes. Serve with sriracha.

Haiku to Sriracha

Almost as much as
your flavor, I love how your
ingredients are

listed in no less
than 5 different languages
on the back of your

bottle. I love how
you need no commercials to
spread the word for you,

because your taste does
the talking. I love how your
most popular brand

in the US (Huy
Fong) is named after the ship
that its founder took

from Vietnam to
the United States. I love
the story of how,

before he came to
the United states, he made
the sauce in Gerber

baby food jars. But
I hate to think of any
child whose parent might

have fed them this by
accident. It's a long way
from mashed bananas.

Dessert

July 4th Cherry Pie

Ingredients: 2
cups of flour, ½ teaspoon
of salt, 2/3 cup

of shortening, 6
or 7 tablespoons of
water, 32

ounces of sour
cherries, 3/4 cup of
sugar, 1/4

cup of corn starch, 1
tablespoon of margarine,
& 1 or even

2 heaping teaspoons
almond extract, depending
on the fruit's tartness

Directions: To make the crust, mix in

a bowl the flour & salt. Cut in the shortening

until the pieces are smaller than a marble.

Gradually add the water & stir until

the dough comes together. Divide into two balls.

On a lightly floured surface, roll

one of the balls until you've got

a disc (It should be about a foot

in diameter.) Transfer this to a pie plate,

& press down to conform to its shape.

Roll the rest of the dough & cut into inch-wide

strips. (These will go on top of the pie

as a lattice.) So, there's your crust.

Now, for the filling: first, you must

find a cherry tree. Don't chop it down. Instead,

just pick the cherries. Then pit & drain

them, reserving a cup of liquid. In a saucepan

combine the sugar & cornstarch. Stir in the liquid

& cook over medium heat until slightly

thickened. Remove the pan from the stove & add your

margarine, almond extract, & cherries. Now pour

the entire mixture into the pie

plate. Top with a lattice crust, weaving or not (it

depends on how much coffee you've had).

Cover the edges of the pie with foil & bake at

375° for 25 minutes.

Remove foil & bake for 25 more minutes.

Serve with ice cream, as if that weren't obvious.

As Close to Heaven As You're Gonna Get* Chocolate Cupcake

Ingredients for the Cupcake: 1 cup rice milk, 1 teaspoon apple

cider vinegar, 1 cup sugar (brown is best), 1/3 cup (or a

touch more) canola oil, 1 1/2 teaspoons vanilla extract,

1 cup of flour, 1/3 cup cocoa powder, 3/4 teaspoon

of baking soda, 1/2 teaspoon of baking powder, 1/4

teaspoon of salt, & a half an hour of free time before dessert

*Just kidding: I know that you're a perfect angel. (I don't count weekends.)

**Ingredients for
Chocolate Frosting**: 1 package
of silken tofu,

1/4 cup of
milk, 2 tablespoons syrup,
1 heaping teaspoon

vanilla extract,
a 12 oz package semi-
sweet chocolate chips

Directions for the Cupcake: Preheat

      the oven to 350°. Line a muffin

pan with paper liners. (If you've got

      polka dot liners, these cupcakes taste better in

them. If not, plain will do. But no frilly

      liners. They're just not appetizing. You hear me?

No frills!) In a large bowl, whisk together the milk

      & vinegar. (& don't worry

when it curdles. That's supposed to happen.)

      Add the oil, vanilla extract, & sugar,

& beat the mixture until it foams. In

      a separate bowl, sift together the flour,

cocoa powder, baking soda, baking powder,

& salt. Add this to the other

ingredients & mix until no giant

lumps remain. Pour the mixture into

liners, & bake for 18-20 minutes.

Let cool (if you want to prove that you

have willpower). Or don't (if you're smart). **Directions**

for the Chocolate Frosting: Place the tofu,

milk, syrup, & vanilla in

a blender & puree until smooth.

Meanwhile, melt the chocolate chips in

a metal bowl over a pan of boiling

water. Combine the chocolate with the tofu. Chill, then

spread on top of your cupcakes. **Extra astonishing**

bonus snack: Since you used no eggs, you can lick the

pan with no fear of salmonella.

Pignoli Almond Cookies

Ingredients: 6 or 7 ounces almond paste, 1/8 teaspoon

salt, 1/2 teaspoon baking powder, 1/2 cup of sugar, 1/2

cup slightly softened butter, 1/2 teaspoon of almond extract, 1

cup sifted flour, 1/3 cup of pine nuts, 3 tablespoons rice milk

Directions: Preheat the oven
to 325°. Place 2 slips of parchment paper
on a couple baking sheets. Pulse the almond
paste, & salt, & baking powder,

& 1/3 cup of sugar in a food processor
for 1 minute. In another
bowl, mix the butter & the rest of the sugar
until fluffy. (You can either

time yourself & do this for 3 minutes, or you
can simply mix & mix until
your wrist feels less floppy than a stalk of two-
week-old celery but a little

firmer than a five-year-old dish rag.) Add
the almond paste mixture & almond

extract & beat again. (I know, by

       now your wrist needs a cast. Trust me, it's

worth it, even if you need to pay

       someone to lift these to your mouth for you.) Sift

in the flour & beat again (*"Again?"*) (Deal

       with it.) until you have a crumbly

but soft dough. Pour the pine nuts into a small

       bowl & complete the assembly

line by pouring the milk into another. Now, scoop

       up a tablespoon of dough, & roll it in

your palms until you have a ball. Dip

       one side into the milk, then flatten into the pine

nuts. Place the cookies on the baking sheet

& bake for 14 minutes. Let cool. Eat.

Ricotta Cheese with Honey & Berries

Ingredients: 2
cups of ricotta cheese, 4
ounces of cream cheese,

3 tablespoons of
sugar, 3 tablespoons of
honey, 1 teaspoon

of vanilla extract,
2 cups of strawberries, 2
cups of blueberries,

1 tablespoon of
lemon juice (or more if you
like your desserts tart)

Directions: In a bowl, mix half the sugar,

the ricotta cheese, cream cheese, honey,

& vanilla. (Hey, get your finger

out of that bowl! I mean... you're free

to do what you like, but if you taste now, I bet

you'll just be eating plain berries later.

Not that there's anything wrong with that...)

Cover & place in the refrigerator

for an hour or so. Meanwhile, in a

large bowl, mix the berries with the lemon juice

& the last of the sugar. When the ricotta

mixture is sufficiently cool, scoop

it into bowls & top with the berries. Serve cold.

This recipe pairs well with another bowl.

Quintuple Cheese Plate (& More!)

Ingredients: sliced
baguette, grapes, toasted almonds,
apricot chutney,

goat cheese (try Humboldt
Fog or Blue Ledge), Camembert,
St. Andre Triple

Cream, Cabot Clothbound
Cheddar, a Stilton Blue Cheese,
& a Zinfandel

Directions: On a large platter

or cutting board, arrange the cheeses, interspersed

with a couple piles of the sliced

baguette, the grapes, toasted almonds &/or

a bowl of the chutney. (& make sure

that you tell every guest that the word

"chutney" comes from the Sanskrit verb

"to lick," or the party will be a failure.

This has been scientifically proven,

but not at my house.) Arrange the cheeses

from the mildest to the strongest, & advise

your friends to hold off on the zin

until they've reached some of the later

cheeses, or the wine can overwhelm the flavors.

Drinks

The Elixir of Life

Ingredients: 4 tablespoons elderberry syrup, 3 shots of

freezer-cold vodka, 2 cups tonic water, 2 tablespoons lemon

juice, 2 tablespoons of balsamic vinegar, teaspoon of honey

Directions: First, it's no mistake that this recipe

tastes best at the tail end of summer,

when the majority of elderberries

are touching the ground with the weight of their

abundance. But please, enjoy this cocktail

any time of year. (It's not like the recipe

requires seasonal ingredients like snowballs

or anything. For such requirements, please

see pages 103 & 105.) In

a cocktail shaker, mix the tonic water,

elderberry syrup, vodka, lemon

juice, vinegar, & honey. Makes 2 drinks, so pour

the mixture into 2 glasses, & before you sip

A) make a friend & B) share with him/her. Bottoms up!

Winter Solst on Ice

Ingredients: 2
snowballs the size of golfballs,
(see directions if

it's too hot for things
like snowballs) 2 shots vodka,
a tablespoon lemon

juice, a teaspoon of
maple bitters. Garnish with
a fresh sprig of thyme.

Warning: This & the following drink betray

a distinctly northern bias. Both must

be made in colder climates. Sorry,

Florida! (Another option is just

to manufacture snowballs in your freezer. Then

they're geographically equal-

opportunity recipes.) **Directions:**

Roll a few sprigs of thyme up in a snowball,

& place the snowball at the bottom of a wide

glass. Mix the vodka, lemon juice & bitters.

Swirl them in the glass a few times. Find

a comfy chair & a fireplace (the chair's

optional, the fireplace isn't) Put your feet

up & take a deep sip. Repeat.

Sugar on Snow

Ingredients: 1
well-packed snowball, 1-2
tablespoons maple

syrup (depending
on the size of your sweet tooth),
1/4 teaspoon

of shaved cinnamon,
2 shots bourbon, 1/4
cup tonic water

Directions: Find a clean bank of snow

that has not yet been defiled by people who

are making Winter Solst on Ice

cocktails (see page 103 for advice

on that one). Make 8 snowballs, each slightly larger

than a golf ball. Throw 5 of them at your

neighbor as he shovels his driveway.

(You can use 6 if you have bad aim.)

Bring the other 2 inside & drop them in

2 wide glasses. Mix in the cinnamon,

bourbon, & tonic water. Swirl

until the ingredients are combined. Drizzle

on the syrup, then treat yourself to a taste

to forget about your own un-shoveled driveway.

Mazel Tov Cocktail

Ingredients: 2 tablespoons of turmeric juice, 1 cup switchel,

1 shot of Root (from Art in the Age Spirits), 1 shot ginger liqueur,

1/4 cup of tonic water. Swirl with a handful of ice cubes.

Directions: First, make the turmeric juice by blending 3 tablespoons of water with 1/2 inch of fresh turmeric root (or you can simply mix powdered turmeric with water). Then mix the juice with the switchel, the Root, the ginger liqueur & the tonic water. Pour into a glass with the handful of ice cubes (number of ice cubes will depend on size of hand).

Note: Despite the name, this tastes no better on Rosh Hashana or Hanukkah than on any other day of the year.

Let's face it. It's never the wrong time to drink to life, so *L'chaim!*

Old Bay Bloody Mary

Ingredients: 2
cups of tomato juice, 2
tablespoons lemon

juice, 1 teaspoon of
soy sauce, 1/4 teaspoon
horseradish, 2 shots

vodka, 1 teaspoon
Old Bay, celery stalks for
garnish, a hammock

Directions: Pre-chill a glass (or 4)

in the freezer. Combine the tomato

juice, the lemon juice, the soy sauce, the Old

Bay, & the horseradish. Refrigerate for

a couple hours to let the flavors commingle.

Remove from fridge & mix in your

vodka. Pour a third of the mixture

into a pre-chilled glass, & insert a single

celery stalk for garnish. Serve with ice, a sunny

day, & a hammock. If a book is

involved (one should be) be sure to practice

your balancing skills. Resting the glass carefully

against your side is recommended, but

squeezing it between your thighs is not.

Haiku to Old Bay

Mustard, paprika,
celery, salt, bay leaf, black
pepper, crushed pepper

flakes, nutmeg, allspice,
cloves, cardamom, & ginger:
oh, how I love your

combination. Your
recipe was developed
in the Chesapeake

Bay area in
the 1930s, when crabs
were so plentiful

that some bars gave them
away for free. Seasonings
such as this were said

to have been made to
encourage patrons to drink.
It worked. It stills works.

Index

Notes

I am indebted to many talented chefs and cookbook writers, especially the following:

Isa Chandra Moskowitz and Terry Hope Romero. Skillet Home Fries, Vegan Broccoli Quiche, Practically Perfect Potato Pancakes, The Only Tofu Scram Recipe You'll Ever Need, Mushroom Tomato & Quinoa Stuffed Peppers, Chocolate Cupcake with Chocolate Frosting, and Pignoli Almond Cookies are adapted from their books *Vegan Brunch, Vegan with a Vengeance, Vegan Cookies Invade Your Cookie Jar,* and *Vegan Cupcakes Take Over the World.*

Eggs Italiano and Wheat Berry & Black Bean Chili are adapted from recipes found in *EatingWell* March/April 2007. Mushroom and Bok Choy Hotpot is adapted from a recipe in Winter 2004.

Truly Unruly Tabouli is from adapted from *The Candle Cafe Cookbook,* by Joy Pierson and Bart Potenza with Barbara Scott-Goodman, 2003.

It's All Greek to Me Salad is adapted from a *Bon Appétit* recipe, April 2003.

Tomato & Black Bean Salsa is adapted from an Emeril Lagasse recipe on *Food Network.*

Tomato-Basil Bruschetta is adapted from *Vegetarian Appetizers* by Paulette Mitchel, Chronicle Books, 2001.

Magic Dhal is adapted from *Ethnic Cuisine,* Elizabeth Rozin, Penguin Books, 1983.

Dragon Sauce is adapted from the recipe of *Aux Vivres* in Montreal.

I'd like to thank Bob Heiser for his black bean hummus recipe,

and Jesse Bridges for his family's Eggplant Parm recipe. Our backyard barbecues wouldn't be the same without them!

The Elixir of Life, the Winter Solst on Ice, the Sugar on Snow, & the Mazel Tov Cocktail were all created by mixologist extraordinaire, Joanna Grossman.